VERY
JOKES

Very Rude
JOKES

Stephen Cordwell

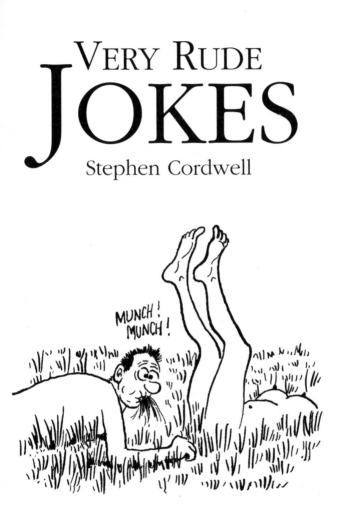

Grange BOOKS

Front cover and inside illustrations by
Fess

Published in 2004 by
Grange Books
An imprint of Grange Books Plc
The Grange
Kingsnorth Industrial Estate
Hoo, nr Rochester
Kent ME3 9ND
www.grangebooks.co.uk

ISBN 1 84013 699 5

Printed in China

Introduction

Jokes are a reflection of culture and national perspective, and as such, vary enormously from country to country. What seems funny in one part of the world may not seem so in another. But, curiously, dirty jokes seem to be pretty universal. The odds are that the one that makes an Englishman laugh will also tickle the ribs of a Russian or a Chinaman.

Perhaps it is because the one thing everyone has in common is the human body and its most basic functions: sex and the latter part of the digestive process. Most nations share a sense of privacy about such things, so when they are aired publicly the response is a strange mixture of shock, embarrassment, relief and recognition. The last of these is particularly important because the listener must be familiar enough with the context to create for themselves a visual image of the events described in the gag. The sudden, and hopefully unexpected, combination of these elements usually results in the explosive event we call laughter.

Dirty jokes have a long, illustrious history in our oral and written heritage, and crude language is an integral part of the telling. Sex is a three-letter word that often needs some old-fashioned four-letter words to convey its full meaning. The breach of this particular social taboo is an integral part of a concept designed to sabotage the constraints of polite society. Somewhere in all our hearts lies the seed of revolution. Even if this is all bollocks…dirty jokes are funny!

SLIGHTLY RUDE JOKES

A middle-aged husband comes home one night to his crying wife. He asks her what's wrong. As she stares into the mirror, she sobs, "Look at me – my hair's getting grey, my boobs aren't perky, and my ass, hips and thighs are all flabby. I feel just horrible. Tell me something that will make me feel better." The husband replies, "Well, there's nothing wrong with your eyesight."

• • •

A young boy goes to the zoo with his father. As they are passing the elephant enclosure, the youngster looks over at a big bull elephant. After a few seconds he turns to his father and asks, "Dad, what's that hanging down from the elephant?" His father replies, "That's his trunk, Son." "No, no, Dad," says the boy, "there, at the back." "Oh, that's his tail." replies his father. "No, Dad," the exasperated boy snaps, "there, between his legs."
The father looks over and replies, "Why, that's his penis, Son."
The young lad thinks about the answer for a minute, and then says to his father, "That's funny. When I was here last week, Mommy told me that it was nothing." "Well, Son," replies his father, "you have to remember that your mother is a very spoiled woman."

A man was so proud of the fact that his wife had given birth to seven children that he began to call her "mother of seven" rather than by her first name. The wife was amused at first, but a few months later she had grown tired of her husband's habit. "Mother of seven!" he would say, "where's my blue shirt?" "Hey, mother of seven! What's for dinner tonight?" This persisted despite her complaints and was gradually driving her crazy.

At last, while attending a party with her husband, he shouted across the crowded room, "Hey, mother of seven! I think it's time to go." The wife spotted her moment and shouted back, "I'll be right with you – father of five!"

• • •

An elderly gentleman was sitting on a bench at the mall. A sullen punk slouched to the bench and sat down. His hair was an impressive array of tall spikes dyed a crazy rainbow of colours. The old man couldn't help but stare. Every time the young man looked his way, the old man was staring. Irritated, the punk finally sneered sarcastically, "What's the matter, you old fart? Have you never done anything wild in your life?"

Without batting an eye, the old bloke replied, "I got very drunk in Panama once and had sex with a parrot...I was just wondering if you were my son."

• • •

A young woman married and had 13 children before her husband died. A year later, she married again and had seven more children. Again, her husband died. But again she remarried, and this time had five more children. Sadly, her own time came and she passed away. Standing before her coffin, the preacher prayed to the Lord, thanking him for this loving woman who fulfilled his commandment to 'Go forth and multiply' so enthusiastically.
In his final eulogy, he ended with the words, "Thank you Lord, for they are finally together." Leaning over to his neighbour, one mourner asked, "Do you think he means her first, second or third husband?" The other mourner then replied, "I think he means her legs."

• • •

Jack was tired of his wife's extravagance and suggested that she get a part-time job. But without any particular skills to offer, they couldn't come up with a solution. At last Jack said, "Well, to get you started, I'll put a pound in your piggy bank each time we make love."

The weeks passed, and he started to wonder how much she had accumulated and decided to open the piggy bank. Out came a cluster of pound coins and a large number of five, ten and even twenty-pound notes. He called to his wife and asked where the notes had come from. "Well," she pouted, "not everyone's as stingy as you!"

• • •

I was happy. My girlfriend and I had been dating for over a year, and so we decided to get married. My parents helped us in every way, my friends encouraged me, and as for my girlfriend – she was a dream! There was only one thing bothering me – very much indeed – and that one thing was her younger sister.

My prospective sister-in-law was 20 years of age, wore tight miniskirts and low-cut blouses. She would regularly bend down when quite near me and I got many a pleasant view of her underwear. It had to be deliberate. She never did it when she was near anyone else.

One day, little sister called and asked me to come over to check the wedding invitations. She was alone when I arrived. She whispered to me that she had feelings and desires for me that she couldn't overcome and didn't really want to overcome. She told me that she wanted to make love to me just once before I got married and committed my life to her sister.

I was in total shock and couldn't believe what she had just told me. She said, "I'm going upstairs to my bedroom, and if you want to go ahead with it just come up and get me." I was stunned. I was unable to speak as I watched her go up the stairs. When she reached the top she pulled down her panties and tossed them down to me.

I stood there for a moment, then turned and went straight to the front door. I opened the door and stepped out of the house. I walked straight towards my car. My future father-in-law was standing outside. With tears in his eyes he hugged me and said, "We are so happy that you have passed our little test. We couldn't ask for a better man for our daughter. Welcome to the family."

The moral of this story is: always keep your condoms in the car.

• • •

An elderly couple were celebrating their 50th wedding anniversary and they decided to go back to the beautiful little village where they first met. Inside the cosy pub they used to frequent, the man said to the woman, "Remember the field where we first made love? I propped you up against the fence." She nodded her head, "Oh, yes, I do. Let's go there and do it again – just for old time's sake."

Out of sight from them, the local policeman was in the next booth and heard the conversation. He thought he'd better follow them and make sure no one disturbed them. The couple got to the field, took off their clothes and the man pressed the woman against the fence. From the bushes the policeman watched in amazement. Arms and legs were flying everywhere, accompanied by breathless moans and cries. He had never seen such wild lovemaking. After five minutes they fell to the ground, covered in sweat and breathing heavily. Then they slowly stood up and got dressed.

As the couple made their way back to the car, the policeman stepped out and said, "I just followed you to make sure no one bothered you. But I have to say, that was the most wonderful lovemaking I've ever seen. You must have been a wild couple when you were young." "Not really," replied the old man. "When we were young that fence wasn't electric."

• • •

An Englishman and a Frenchman were hunting in the woods together when a gorgeous and totally naked blonde girl ran through a clearing ahead of them. "Mon Dieu!" cried the Frenchman. "How I would love to eat that. Oh, yes!" So the Englishman shot her.

• • •

A dying women called her husband and asked him to take out the wooden box that she kept under the bed. He did so, and then opened it as she requested. He found £6,700 in cash, but was puzzled by the three eggs he also saw in the box, so he asked his wife what the eggs were for. "Oh, those," she replied. "Well, every time we had crappy sex, I put an egg in the box." The husband smiled as he thought to himself that after 35 years of marriage that wasn't bad going. Then he asked, "But what about the £6,700?" "Oh, that," she replied. "Every time I got a dozen I sold them."

• • •

Doctor Dave had slept with one of his patients and felt guilty all day long. No matter how much he tried to forget about it, he couldn't. The guilt and sense of betrayal was overwhelming. But every once in a while he'd hear a reassuring voice inside his head that said, "Dave, don't worry about it. You aren't the first medical practitioner to sleep with one of their patients, and you won't be the last. You've had no complaint and you're single. Just let it go."

But invariably, another voice would bring him back to reality, whispering, "...but Dave – you're a vet!"

• • •

One dismal rainy night, a taxi driver spotted an arm waving from the shadows of an alley halfway down the block. Even before he rolled to a stop, a woman leapt into the cab and slammed the door. Checking his rear-view mirror as he pulled away, he was startled to see a dripping wet, naked woman sitting on the back seat. "Where to?" he stammered. "The railway station," answered the woman. "OK," he said, taking another long glance in the mirror.

The woman caught him staring and asked, "And what the hell are you looking at, driver?" "Well, ma'am, I noticed that you're completely naked, and I was just wondering how you intended to pay your fare," he replied. The woman spread her legs, put her feet up on the front seat, smiled at the driver and said, "Does this answer your question?" Still looking in the mirror, the driver asked, "Haven't you got anything smaller?"

• • •

A lady walked into a pharmacy and spoke to the pharmacist. She asked, "Do you stock Viagra?" "Yes, we do," the pharmacist answered. "Does it really work?" she smiled. "Oh, certainly," he answered. "So, can you get it over the counter?" she asked. "I can if I take two," came the reply.

• • •

One Monday morning a postman is walking the neighbourhood on his usual round. As he approaches one of the homes, he notices that the owner's car is in the driveway. Jim, the homeowner, coming out with a load of empty beer and liquor bottles, cuts his curiosity short.

"Wow, Jim, looks like you guys had a hell of a party last night," the postman comments. Jim, in

16

obvious pain replies, "Actually we had it Saturday night, this is the first time I have felt like moving since 4 am Sunday morning. We had about fifteen couples from around the neighbourhood over for the party and things got a bit wild. Heck, we even got so drunk that around midnight we started playing WHO AM I?"

The postman thinks a moment and asks, " How do you play that?"

Jim continues between hungover moans, "Well, all the guys go in the bedroom, and we come out one at a time covered by a sheet with only our 'tackle' showing through a hole in the sheet. Then the women try to guess who it is."

The postman laughs and says, "Damn, I'm sorry I missed that." "Probably a good thing you did," Jim grunts, "your name was guessed five times."

• • •

80-year-old Bessie bursts into the recreation room at the retirement home. She holds her clenched fist in the air and announces, "Anyone who can guess what's in my hand can have sex with me tonight!" An elderly gentleman in the rear shouts out, "An elephant?" Bessie thinks for a minute and says, "Close enough."

• • •

The doctor said, "Joe, the good news is I can cure your headaches. The bad news is that it will require castration. You have a very rare condition which causes your testicles to press up against the base of your spine, and the pressure creates one hell of a headache. The only way to relieve the pressure is to remove the testicles."

Joe was shocked and depressed. He wondered if he had anything to live for. He couldn't concentrate long enough to answer, but decided he had no choice but to go under the knife. When he left the hospital he was without a headache for the first time in 20 years, but he felt like he was missing an important part of himself.

As he walked down the street, he realized that he felt like a different person. He could make a new beginning and live a new life. He saw a men's clothing store and thought, "That's what I need – a new suit." He entered the shop and told the salesman, "I'd like a new suit." The elderly tailor eyed him briefly and said, "Let's see...size 44 long." Joe laughed, "That's right, how did you know?" "Been in the business 60 years!" replied the tailor.

Joe tried on the suit. It fitted perfectly. As Joe admired himself in the mirror, the salesman asked, "How about a new shirt?" Joe thought for a moment and then said, "Sure." The salesman eyed Joe and said, "Let's see...34 sleeve and 16 and a half neck." Joe was surprised, "That's right, how did you know?" "Been in the business 60 years!" the tailor smiled. Joe tried on the shirt, and it fitted perfectly. As Joe adjusted the collar in the mirror, the salesman asked, "How about new shoes?" Joe was on a roll and said, "Sure." The salesman eyed Joe's feet and said, "Let's see...9-E." Joe was astonished, "That's right, how did you know?" "Been in the business 60 years!" said the tailor. Joe tried on the shoes and they fitted perfectly.

Joe walked comfortably around the shop and the salesman asked, "How about some new underwear?" Joe thought for a second and said, "Sure." The salesman stepped back, eyed Joe's waist and said, "Let's see...size 36." Joe laughed, "Ah ha! I got you! I've worn size 34 since I was 18 years old." The salesman shook his head, "You can't wear a size 34. A 34 underwear would press your testicles up against the base of your spine and give you one hell of a headache."

• • •

A husband and wife are travelling by car from Edinburgh to Esher. After almost 24 hours on the road, they're too tired to continue, and they decide to stop for a rest. They stop at a nice hotel and take a room, but they only plan to sleep for four hours. When they check out four hours later, the desk clerk hands them a bill for £350. The man explodes and demands to know why the charge is so high. He tells the clerk that although it's a nice hotel, the rooms certainly aren't worth £350. When the clerk tells him £350 is the standard rate, the man insists on speaking to the manager.

The manager appears, listens to the man, and then explains that the hotel has an Olympic-sized pool and a huge conference centre that were available for the husband and wife to use. "But we didn't use them," the man complains. "Well, they are here, and you could have," explains the manager. He goes on to explain they could have taken in one of the shows for which the hotel is famous. "The best entertainers from New York, London and Paris perform here," the manager says. "But we didn't go to any of those shows," complains the man again. "Well, we have them, and you could have," the manager replies.

No matter what facility the manager mentions, the man replies, "But we didn't use it!" The manager is unmoved, and eventually the man gives up and agrees to pay. He writes a cheque and gives it to the manager. The manager is surprised when he looks at the cheque. "But sir," he says, "this cheque is only made out for £100." "That's right," says the man. "I charged you £250 for sleeping with my wife." "But I didn't!" exclaims the manager. "Well," the man replies, "she was here, and you could have."

• • •

Two Scottish nuns had just arrived in the US by boat when one said to the other, "I heard that the occupants of this country actually eat dogs." "Odd," her companion replied, "but if we are to live in America, we should do as the Americans do." Nodding emphatically, the Mother Superior pointed to a hot dog vendor and they both walked towards it.

"Two dogs, please," said one. The vendor was only too pleased to oblige and he wrapped both hot dogs in foil. Excited, the nuns hurried over to a bench and began to unwrap their 'dogs'. The Mother Superior was first to open hers. She stared at it for a moment, then leaned over to the other nun and whispered cautiously, "What part did you get?"

• • •

Hung Chow calls in to work and says, "Hey, Boss, I not come work today, I really sick. I got headache, stomach ache and my legs hurt. I not come work." The boss says, "You know, Hung

Chow, I really need you today. When I feel like this I go to my wife and tell her to give me sex. That makes everything better and I can go to work. You should try that." Two hours later Hung Chow calls again: "Boss, I do what you say and feel great. Thank you. I be at work soon. Hey, you got nice house."

● ● ●

A man comes home to his wife one evening with a big bunch of flowers. Flattered but wary, she says, "I suppose this means I have to get on my back with my legs open." "Oh, come on!" sighs the husband, "I can't believe that we don't have a single vase in this house?"

● ● ●

A man boards an aeroplane and takes his seat. As he settles in, he glances up and sees a most beautiful woman boarding the plane. He soon realises she is heading straight towards his seat. A wave of nervous anticipation washes over him. Lo and behold, she takes the seat right beside his. Eager to strike up a conversation, he blurts out, "Business trip or vacation?" "Nymphomaniac Convention in Milan," she states. Whoa!!! He swallows hard and is instantly crazed with excitement. Here's the most gorgeous woman he has ever seen, sitting RIGHT next to him and she's going to a meeting of nymphomaniacs!

Struggling to maintain his outward cool, he calmly asks, "What's your business role at this convention?" "Lecturer," she says. "I use my experiences to debunk some of the popular myths about sexuality." "Really?" he says, swallowing hard. "What myths are those?" "Well," she explains, "one popular myth is that black men are the most well-endowed when, in fact, it is the Native American Indian who is most likely to possess that trait. Another popular myth is that French men are the best lovers, when actually it is men of Greek descent."

Suddenly, the woman becomes very embarrassed and blushes. "I'm sorry," she says, "I shouldn't be discussing this with you, I don't even know your name!" "Tonto," the man says, as he extends his hand, "Tonto Papadopoulos."

• • •

Two guys sneak into a farmer's fruit garden and start helping themselves to the fruit. The farmer spots them from his window and comes out with a shotgun. "Since you guys like fruit so much, go pick 100 of which ever fruit you want," says the farmer. The first guy decides to pick grapes. When he gets 100 he goes back to the farmer, who tells him, "Now shove 'em all up your arse." The guy gets all 100 up his ass. He feels extremely uncomfortable, but then he starts to laugh. "Why are you laughing?" asked the farmer. The man replies, "My friend is out picking watermelons!"

• • •

A newly married farmer is giving his wife last-minute instructions before heading to town to collect some urgent supplies. "The chap from the insemination service will be along this afternoon to impregnate one of the cows. I've hung a nail by the right stall so you'll know which is the right cow."

He goes over the instructions to make absolutely sure that she understands, then gets in his truck and sets off for town. An hour later the expected man from the insemination service arrives, so the wife takes him out to the barn and leads him directly to the stall with the nail. She points to the place and says, "This is the cow right here." "Right you are," he smiles. "And so what's the nail for?" The wife shrugs and says, "I suppose it's to hang your pants on."

• • •

A successful rancher died and left everything to his devoted wife. She was a very good-looking woman, and determined to keep the ranch, but knew she could not handle it by herself, so she decided to place an ad in the newspaper for a ranch hand. Two men applied for the job. One was gay and the other a drunk. She thought long and hard about it, and when no one else applied, she decided to hire the gay guy, figuring it would be safer to have him around the ranch than the drunk.

The hired man proved to be a hard worker who put in long hours every day and, luckily, knew a lot about ranching. For weeks, the two of them worked hard putting the ranch back in shape, and their hard work paid off because the ranch was doing very well. Then one day, the rancher's widow said to the hired hand, "You've done a really wonderful job and the ranch looks great. You deserve a day off. You ought to go into town and let off a little steam – kick up your heels a bit." The hired hand readily agreed, and went into town one Saturday night.

However, one o'clock came and he didn't return. Two o'clock and still no sign of the hired hand, and the rancher's widow started to worry. Finally, he showed up around two-thirty in the morning, and upon entering the ranch house he found the rancher's widow sitting by the fireplace, a glass of wine in her hand, waiting for him. She quietly called him over.

"Unbutton my blouse and take it off," she said.

Trembling, he did as she directed. "Now take off my boots." He did as she asked, ever so slowly. "Now take off my stockings." He removed each one gently and placed them neatly by her boots. "Now take off my skirt." He slowly unbuttoned it, watching her eyes in the firelight. "Now take off my bra." Again with trembling hands he did as he was told. "Now," she said, "take off my panties." By the light of the fire, he slowly took them off.

Then she looked at him and said, "If you ever wear my clothes into town again, I'll fire you on the spot."

• • •

An elderly man walks into a confessional and tells the priest, "I am 92 years old, and have a wonderful wife of 70 years, and many children, grandchildren and great grandchildren. Yesterday, I picked up two college girls, hitchhiking. We went to a motel, where I had sex with each of them three times."

Priest: Are you sorry for your sins?
Man: What sins?
Priest: What kind of a Catholic are you?
Man: I'm Jewish.
Priest: Then why are you telling me all this?
Man: I'm telling everybody.

After a few years of married life, a man finds that he is unable to perform. He goes to his doctor, who tries a few things but nothing seems to work. So the doctor refers him to a witch doctor. The witch doctor says, "I can cure this." He throws a white powder in a flame, and there is a flash with billowing blue smoke.

Then he says, "This is powerful healing, but you can only use it once a year. All you have to do is say '123', and it shall rise for as long as you wish!" The guy then asks, "What happens when it's over, and I don't want to continue?" "All you or your partner has to say is '1234', and it will go down. But be warned: it will not work again for another year," says the witch doctor.

The guy goes home, and that night he is ready to surprise his wife. He showers, shaves and puts on his most exotic after-shave lotion. After he gets into bed and is lying next to her, he says, "123," and suddenly he gets an erection just as the witch doctor said. His wife, who is facing the other way, turns over and says, "What did you say '123' for?"

• • •

Two Indians and a hillbilly were walking in the woods when one of the Indians ran up a hill to the mouth of a small cave. "Wooooo! Wooooo!

Wooooo!" he called into the cave, and then he listened very closely until he heard an answering, "Wooooo! Wooooo! Wooooo!" He tore off his clothes and ran into the cave.

The hillbilly was puzzled and asked the other Indian what was going on. The other Indian replied, "It is our custom during mating season when Indian men see cave, they holler 'Wooooo! Wooooo! Wooooo!' into the opening. If they get an answer back, it means there is a girl in there waiting to mate."

Just then they saw another cave. The Indian ran up to the opening of the cave, stopped, and hollered, "Wooooo! Wooooo! Wooooo!" Immediately, there was an answering "Wooooo! Wooooo! Wooooo!" from deep inside the cave. He tore off his clothes and ran into the cave.

The hillbilly wandered around in the woods alone for a while, and then he came upon a huge cave. As he looked in amazement at the size of the opening, he was thinking, "Whoa, man! Look at the size of this cave! It is bigger than those the Indians found. There must be some really big, fine women in this cave!"

He stood in front of the opening and hollered

with all his might, "Wooooo! Wooooo! Wooooo!" He grinned and closed his eyes, praying in anticipation until then he heard, "WOOOOOOOOO! WOOOOOOOOO! WOOOOOOOOO!"

With a gleam in his eyes and a smile on his face, he tore off his clothes and raced into the cave. The following day, the headline of the local newspaper read: NAKED HILLBILLY RUN OVER BY TRAIN.

• • •

Charles is seeing three women on a regular basis and can't decide which to marry. A friend suggests that he sets them a test, and Charles decides that this is a great idea. He gives each woman a present of £1,000 to see what she will do with the money. The first goes for a total makeover. She goes to a top beauty salon, then a famous hairdresser and finally buys an expensive new outfit for their next meeting. She tells him that she has done this to be more attractive for him because she loves him so much. Charles is impressed.

The second goes shopping and spends all the money on gifts for Charles. She gets him a new set of golf clubs, a top quality laptop and some expensive clothes. As she shows him these gifts, she tells him that she has spent all the money on him because she loves him so much. Again, he is impressed.

The third invests the money in the stock market. She earns several times the original £1,000. She gives him back his £1,000 and reinvests the remainder in a joint account. She tells him that she wants to save for their future because she loves him so much. Obviously, Charles is extremely impressed. He thinks for several minutes about what each woman has done with the money, then picks up the phone and proposes to the one with the biggest tits.

• • •

Two guys are moving about in a supermarket when their carts collide. The first one says to the other, "Sorry about that, I'm looking for my wife, and I guess I wasn't watching where I was going."

The second guy says, "What a coincidence, I'm looking for my wife, too, and I'm getting a little desperate." The first guy says, "Well, maybe I can help you. What does your wife look like?"

The second guy answers, "She's tall, with red hair, deep blue eyes, long legs, big firm breasts and a tight butt. What does your wife look like?"

To which the first guy replies, "Never mind –
let's look for yours."

• • •

A man whose wife kept chickens bought a young
live cockerel to breed from. He was on his way
home when he remembered that he hadn't got
his key with him, and his wife wasn't due home
for a couple of hours. He decided to kill time by
going to the local cinema. In order to avoid any
trouble getting in, he stuffed the chicken into his
trousers.

Once the show started, he became so engrossed
in the film that he failed to notice that the
chicken had stuck his head out of his fly. Two
women were seated next to him, and one turned
to the other and whispered to her friend, "Look!
Look! There's a cock sticking out of that man's
pants!" Her friend sniffed haughtily and hissed
back, "If you've seen one, you've seen them all."
"True," answered the other woman, "but this
one's eating my popcorn."

• • •

Jim goes to the doctor and says, "Doc, my sex
life is a disaster. I can't seem to get a proper
erection." After a thorough examination, the
doctor tells Jim, "Well, the problem lies in the
fact that the muscles around the base of your
penis are damaged. There's really nothing I can

do for you unless you're willing to subject yourself to an experimental treatment."

Jim asks nervously, "What exactly does this treatment involve?" "Well," the doctor explains, "a surgeon will take muscle tissue from the trunk of a baby elephant and replace the existing muscles in your penis." Jim is quiet for a while, then says, "Well, the thought of going through life without ever having sex again is unbearable. I'm ready to go for it."

Jim goes into the operating theatre, and after a period of convalescence, returns to the doctor for a final check-up. When the examination is over, the doctor pronounces Jim 'healed and ready for action'. Eager to use his experimental equipment, Jim plans a romantic evening for his new girlfriend and takes her to one of the finest restaurants in town, anticipating a glorious conclusion to the evening.

In the middle of the main course he feels a stirring between his legs that continues to the point of being painful. To relieve the pressure, Jim places his napkin on his lap and unzips his fly. His prick immediately springs from confinement, flicking the napkin on to the floor. It curves over his plate, grabs a bread roll and then whips back into his pants! His girlfriend sits stunned. Then a gleam comes into her eye and she whispers, "That was amazing! Please do it again." Jim looks very uncomfortable, then groans, "I'd love to, but I don't think I can fit another roll up my arse."

• • •

A travelling salesman entered a small hotel and noticed a very attractive woman in the foyer giving him the eye. In a casual manner he walked over and started chatting to her as though he had known her all his life. They got on extremely well, and eventually both walked up to the reception desk and registered as man and wife. After two days of unbridled passion, the salesman walked up to the desk and informed the clerk that he was checking out. The clerk presented him with his bill for £1200. "There must be some mistake," he protested. "I have been here only two days." "Yes," replied the clerk, "but your wife has been here a month."

• • •

A grocery shop owner hires a rather attractive young female with a penchant for very short skirts to be his assistant. One day a young man enters the store, glances at the girl, and spots the loaves of bread on a high shelf behind the counter. "I'd like some raisin bread, please," the man says politely. The assistant nods and climbs up a ladder to reach the raisin bread.

The man, standing almost directly beneath her, is provided with an excellent view. As the girl brings down the bread, a small group of male customers gathers around the young man, following his gaze. Soon each person is asking for raisin bread, just to see her climb up and down. After several trips the assistant is tired and irritated. She stops at the top of the ladder, glaring at the men standing below and sees an elderly man who has just entered the shop. "I suppose yours is raisin, too?" she snaps. "Not really," croaks the feeble old man, "but it certainly twitched a couple of times."

88-year-old Dan and 82-year-old Beryl became very attached to each other at their nursing home. Although they didn't have sex, Beryl would go to Dan's room every evening, where they would lie together in bed and watch TV while she gently held his penis. One night Beryl went into Dan's room and found another resident of the nursing home in Dan's bed, watching TV and holding his prick.

"Dan!" wailed Beryl, "is she prettier than me?" Dan replied, "NO!" "Does she have a nicer personality?" Dan replied, "NO!" "Then please tell me what does she have that I don't?" "Parkinson's," Dan replied.

• • •

RUDE JOKES

A lonely older woman decided it was time to get married. She put a want ad in the local paper: 'HUSBAND WANTED. Must be in my age group, must not beat me, must not run around on me, and must still be good in bed! All applicants must apply in person'. Next day, she heard the doorbell ring. Much to her dismay, when she opened the door, there sat a man in a wheelchair. He had no arms or legs.

She asked coolly, "You're not expecting me to consider you, are you? Just look at you – you have no legs!" The old man smiled, "Therefore no chance to run around on you!" She snorted, "You have no arms either!" Again the old man smiled, "Nor can I beat you!" She raised her eyebrows and gazed at him intensely. "Are you still good in bed?" she asked. He smirked and said, "I rang the doorbell, didn't I?"

• • •

A Greek family is sitting around the supper table, and the son says can he ask a personal question. The father says, "Ask away." The young man asks, "Dad, how many kinds of breasts are there?" The father, surprised, answers, "Well, Son, there are three kinds of breasts. In her twenties, a woman's breasts are like melons, round and firm. In her thirties to forties, they are like pears, still nice but hanging a bit. After fifty, they are like onions." "Onions?" asks the son. "Yes," replies the father, "when you see them, they make you cry."

This infuriates the wife and daughter, so the daughter says, "Can I ask a personal question? Mom, how many kinds of penises are there?" The mother, surprised, smiles, and looks at her husband and answers, "Well, Daughter, a man goes through three phases. In his twenties, a man's penis is like an oak, mighty and hard. In his thirties and forties, it is like a birch, flexible but reliable. After his fifties, it is like a Christmas tree." The daughter looks puzzled. "A Christmas tree?" "Yes," replies the mother, "dead from the root, and the balls are there for decoration only."

• • •

An elderly couple met for a romp in the library of the nursing home. As they undressed and were about to screw, the woman decided to warn the man about her heart condition. "I must tell you," she whispered shyly, "I have acute angina." "Thank God," the man replied, "because your tits are dreadful!"

• • •

An owner of a horse ranch receives a call from a friend, saying he is sending over a midget with a speech impairment who is looking to buy a horse. The midget arrives, and the rancher asks if he would like a male or a female horse. "A female horth," the midget replies. So the rancher shows him his finest filly.

"Nith looking horth. Can I thee her mouf?" So the rancher picks up the midget and shows him the horse's mouth. "Nith mouf. Can I thee her eyeth?" Again, the rancher picks the midget up and shows him the horse's eyes. "OK, what about her earzth?" The rancher, getting pretty pissed off by now, lifts him up higher to the ears. "OK," says the midget, "can I thee her twat?"

With that, the rancher picks up the midget and shoves the little fella's head way up into the filly's twat, then yanks him out. Shaking his head, and out of breath, the midget says, "Perhapth I thould rephrathe that. Can I thee her wun awownd a wittle bit?"

• • •

The sales girl in the Slinky Venus sex boutique didn't bat an eyelid when a customer purchased an artificial vagina. "What are you going to use it for?" she asked. "That's none of your business," answered the customer, beetroot red and thoroughly embarrassed. "Calm down, sir," smiled the salesgirl, "the only reason I'm asking is that if you're going to eat it, there's no VAT."

A girl asks her boyfriend to come over Friday night and have dinner with her parents. Since this is such a big event, the girl announces to her boyfriend that after dinner she would like to go out and make love for the first time. Well, the boy is ecstatic, but he has never had sex before, so he takes a trip to the pharmacist to get some condoms. The pharmacist helps the boy for about an hour. He tells the boy everything there is to know about condoms and sex.

At the counter, the pharmacist asks the boy how many condoms he'd like to buy: a 3-pack, 10-pack or a family pack. "I'm really going to give it to this girl," the boy tells the pharmacist. "I intend to plug every orifice in her body at least twice." The pharmacist, with a laugh, suggests the family pack, saying the boy will be rather busy, it being his first time and all. That night, the boy shows up at the girl's parent's house and meets his girlfriend at the door. "Oh, I'm so excited for you to meet my parents. Come on in!"

The boy goes inside and is taken to the dinner table where the girl's parents are seated. The boy quickly offers to say grace and bows his head. A minute passes, and the boy is still deep in prayer with his head down. Ten minutes pass, and still there is no movement from the boy. Finally, after 20 minutes with his head down, the girlfriend finally leans over and whispers to the boyfriend, "I had no idea you were this religious." The boy turns, and whispers back, "I had no idea your father was a pharmacist!"

• • •

Jack and Jill were about to get married, when Jack's father took him to the side to give him some fatherly advice..."Jack, my son," he began, "when I got married to your mother the first thing I did when we got home was to take off my trousers. I gave them to your mother and told her to try them on, which she did. They were enormous on her and she said to me that she couldn't possibly wear them, as they were too large. I said to her, "Of course they are too large for you. I wear the trousers in this family and I always will. Ever since that day we have never had a single problem."

Jack took his father's advice to heart, and as soon as he got Jill alone after the wedding he did the same thing. He took off his trousers and handed them to Jill and told her to try them on. When she did she said, "I can't wear these, they're far too large for me." "Exactly," Jack replied, "I wear the trousers in this family and I always will. I don't want you to ever forget that." Then Jill took off her knickers and gave them to Jack. "Try these on, Jack," she said, so he tried them on but they were too small. "I can't get into your knickers," said Jack. So Jill said, "Exactly, and if you don't change your f**king attitude, you never will!"

• • •

A man escapes from a prison where he had been kept for 15 years. As he runs away, he finds a house and breaks into it, looking for money and guns, but only finds a young couple in bed. He orders the guy out of bed and ties him up in a chair. While tying the girl up to the bed, he gets on top of her, kisses her on the neck, then gets up and goes to the bathroom.

While he's in there, the husband tells his wife, "Listen, this guy is an escaped prisoner – look at his clothes! He probably spent lots of time in jail, and hasn't seen a woman in years. I saw how he kissed your neck. If he wants sex, don't resist, don't complain, just do what he tells you, just give him satisfaction. This guy must be dangerous. If he gets angry, he'll kill us. Be strong, Honey, I love you."

To which the wife responds, "He was not kissing my neck. He was whispering in my ear. He told me he was gay, thought you were cute, and asked if we kept any Vaseline in the bathroom. Be strong, Honey, I love you, too."

TOP TEN TIMES IN HISTORY WHEN USING THE "F" WORD WAS APPROPRIATE

10th - "Scattered @#$%ing showers, my ass!" - Noah, 4314 BC

9th - "How the @#$% did you work that out?" - Pythagoras, 126 BC

8th - "You want WHAT on the @#$%ing ceiling?" - Michelangelo, 1566

7th - "Where did all those @#$%ing Indians come from?" - Custer, 1877

6th - "It does so @#$%ing look like her!" - Picasso, 1926

5th - "Where the @#$% are we?" - Amelia Earhart, 1937

4th - "Any @#$%ing idiot could understand that." - Einstein, 1938

3rd - "What the @#$% was that?" - Mayor of Hiroshima, 1945

2nd - "I need this parade like I need a @#$%ing hole in the head!" - JFK, 1963

1st - "Aw c'mon. Who the @#$% is going to find out?" - Bill Clinton, 1997

A lady walks into a Mercedes dealership. She browses around, then spots the perfect car and walks over to inspect it. As she bends to feel the fine leather upholstery, a loud fart escapes her. Very embarrassed, she looks around nervously to see if anyone has noticed her little accident and hopes a sales person doesn't pop up right now.

As she turns back, there standing next to her is Andre, a salesman. "Good day, Madame. How may we help you today?" Very uncomfortably she asks, "Sir, what is the price of this lovely vehicle?" He answers, "Madame, I'm very sorry to say that if you farted just touching it, you are going to shit yourself when you hear the price."

• • •

Joe wants to buy a motorcycle. He doesn't have much luck, until, one day, he comes across a beautiful Honda Gold Wing with a 'For Sale' sign on it. The bike seems even more beautiful than a new one, although it is ten years old. It is shiny and in absolutely mint condition. He immediately buys it, and asks the seller how he kept it in such great condition for ten years. "Well, it's quite simple, really," says the seller, "whenever the bike is outside and it's going to rain, rub Vaseline on the chrome. It protects it from the rain." And he hands Joe a jar of Vaseline.

That night, his girlfriend, Sandra, invites him over to meet her parents. Naturally, they take the bike there. But just before they enter the house, Sandra stops him and says, "I have to tell you something about my family before we go in. When we eat dinner, we don't talk. In fact, the first person who says anything during dinner has to do the dishes." "No problem," he says. And in they go.

Joe is shocked. Right smack in the middle of the living room is a huge stack of dirty dishes. In the kitchen is another huge stack of dishes. Piled up on the stairs, in the corridor, everywhere he looks – dirty dishes. They sit down to dinner and, sure enough, no one says a word. As dinner progresses, Joe decides to take advantage of the situation. So he leans over and kisses Sandra. No one says a word. So he reaches over and fondles her breasts.

Still nobody says a word. So he stands up, grabs her, rips her clothes off, throws her on the table, and screws her right there, in front of her parents. His girlfriend is a little flustered, her dad is obviously livid, and her mom horrified when he sits back down, but no one says a word. He looks at her mom. "She's got a great body," he thinks. So he grabs the mom, bends her over the dinner table, and has his way with her every which way right there and then.

Now his girlfriend is furious and her dad is boiling, but still, there is total silence. All of a sudden there is a loud clap of thunder, and it starts to rain. Joe remembers his motorcycle, so he pulls the jar of Vaseline from his pocket. Suddenly the father backs away from the table and shouts, "All right, enough already. I'll do the f**king dishes!"

● ● ●

A man with a bald head and a wooden leg gets invited to a fancy-dress party. He doesn't know what costume to wear to hide his head and his leg so he writes to a fancy-dress company to explain his problem. A few days later he receives a parcel with a note saying:

"Dear Sir, please find enclosed a pirate's outfit. The spotted handkerchief will cover your bald head and with your wooden leg you will be just right for a pirate." The man thinks this is terrible because they have just emphasised his wooden leg, and so he writes a rude letter of complaint. A week passes and he receives another parcel and a note that says:

"Dear Sir, sorry about before, please find enclosed a monk's habit. The long robe will cover your wooden leg and with your bald head you will really look the part." Now the man is really annoyed since they have gone from emphasising his wooden leg to emphasising his bald head, and he writes another rude letter of complaint. A few days later he receives a third parcel and a note that reads:

"Dear Sir, please find enclosed a tin of treacle. Pour the tin of treacle over your bald head, stick your wooden leg up your arse and go as a toffee apple."

• • •

The new Irish marine captain was assigned to an American regiment in a remote post in the Lebanese desert. During his first inspection, he noticed a camel hitched up behind the mess tent. He asked the American sergeant why the camel was kept there.

"Well, sir," came the nervous reply, "as you know, there are 250 men here and no women. And sir, sometimes the men have...m-m-m...urges. That's why we have the camel, sir."

The Irish captain said, "I can't say that I condone this, but I understand about urges, so the camel can stay." About a month later, the captain starts having a real problem with his own urges. Crazy with passion, he asks the American sergeant to bring the camel to his tent. Putting a stool behind the camel, the captain stands on it, pulls down his pants, and has wild, insane sex with the camel. When he is done, he asks the sergeant, "Is that how the Americans do it?" "Uh, no sir," the sergeant replies, "they usually just ride the camel into town where the girls are."

• • •

A divorced man meets his ex-wife's new husband at a party. Later, after knocking back a few drinks, he goes over to the new husband and asks him, "So...how do you like using second-hand stuff?" To which the new husband replies, "It isn't that bad. Past the first three inches, it's all brand new."

• • •

The Inland Revenue send their auditor to a synagogue. The auditor is doing all the checks and then turns to the rabbi and says, "I noticed that you buy a lot of candles." "Yes," answers the rabbi. "Well, Rabbi, what do you do with the candle drippings?" the auditor asks. "A good question," notes the rabbi. "We actually save them up, and when we have enough we send them back to the candle maker, and every now and then they send us a free box of candles."

"Oh," replies the auditor, somewhat disappointed that his unusual question actually has a practical answer. But he thinks he'll ask another awkward question. "Rabbi, what about all these matzo purchases? What do you do with the crumbs from the matzos?" "Ah, yes," replies the rabbi calmly, "we actually collect up all the crumbs from the matzos, and when we have enough, we send them in a box back to the manufacturer and every now and then they send a free box of matzo balls."

"Oh," replies the auditor, thinking how hard it is to fluster the rabbi.
"Well, Rabbi," he goes on, "what do you do with all the foreskins from the circumcisions?" "Yes, here too, we do not waste," answers the rabbi. "What we do is save up all the foreskins, and when we have enough we send them to The Inland Revenue." "The Inland Revenue?" questions the auditor in disbelief. "Ah, yes," replies the rabbi, "Inland Revenue...and about once a year they send us a prick like you."

• • •

In ancient Greece, Socrates was well known for his wisdom. One day the great philosopher came upon an acquaintance who said excitedly, "Socrates, do you know what I just heard about one of your students?"

"Wait a moment," Socrates replied. "Before telling me anything, I'd like you to pass a little test. It's called the Triple Filter Test." "Triple filter?" said the acquaintance. "That's right,"

Socrates continued, "before you talk to me about my student, it might be a good idea to take a moment and filter what you're going to say. The first filter is Truth. Have you made absolutely sure that what you are about to tell me is true?"

"No," the man said, "actually I just heard about it and..." "All right," said Socrates, "so you don't really know if it's true or not. Now let's try the second filter, the filter of Goodness. Is what you are going to tell me about my student something good?" "No, on the contrary..." "So," Socrates continued, "you want to tell me something bad about him, but you're not certain it's true.

You may still pass the test though, because there's one filter left: the filter of Usefulness. Is what you want to tell me about my student going to be useful to me?" "No, not really." "Well," concluded Socrates, "if what you want to tell me is neither true nor good nor even useful, why tell it to me at all?"

This is why Socrates was a great philosopher and held in such high esteem. It also explains why he never found out that Plato was shagging his wife.

• • •

One day Dai the farmer was in town picking up supplies for his farm. He stopped by the hardware store and picked up a bucket and an anvil. Then, he stopped by the livestock dealer to buy a couple of chickens and a goose. However, he now had a problem: how to carry all his purchases home?

The livestock dealer said, "Why don't you put the anvil in the bucket, carry the bucket in one hand, put a chicken under each arm and carry the goose in your other hand?" "Hey, thanks!" the farmer said, and off he went.

While walking he met a young lady who told him she was lost. She asked, "Can you tell me how to get to 123 Wilson Road?" The farmer said, "Well, as a matter of fact, I live at 132 Wilson Road. Let's take my short cut and go down this alley. We'll be there in no time." The young lady said, "How do I know that when we get in the alley you won't hold me up against the wall, pull up my skirt, and ravish me?"

The farmer said, "Holy smokes, lady, I am carrying a bucket, an anvil, two chickens and a goose. How in the world could I possibly hold you up against the wall and do that?" The young lady said, "Set the goose down, cover him with the bucket, put the anvil on top of the bucket and I'll hold the chickens."

A ventriloquist visiting Wales walks into a small village and sees a local sitting on his porch patting his dog. He figures he'll have a little fun, so he says to the Welshman, "Can I talk to your dog?"

Villager: The dog doesn't talk, you stupid git.
Ventriloquist: Hello dog, how's it going mate?
Dog: Doin' alright.
Villager: (look of extreme shock)
Ventriloquist: Is this bloke your owner?
Dog: Yep.
Ventriloquist: How does he treat you?
Dog: Quite well. He walks me twice a day, feeds me great food, and takes me to the lake once a

week to play.

Villager: (look of utter disbelief)

Ventriloquist: Mind if I talk to your horse?

Villager: Uh, the horse doesn't talk either...as far as I know.

Ventriloquist: Hey horse, how's it going?

Horse: Cool.

Villager: (absolutely dumbfounded)

Ventriloquist: Is this your owner?

Horse: Yep.

Ventriloquist: How does he treat you?

Horse: Pretty good. Thanks for asking. He rides me regularly, brushes me down often, and keeps me in the barn to protect me from the weather.

Villager: (total look of amazement)

Ventriloquist: Mind if I talk to your sheep?

Villager: (in a panic) The sheep's a f**king liar!

• • •

A young guy was on his back on a massage table, wearing only a towel over his groin. A young, very attractive Swedish girl was massaging his shoulders, then his chest, and gradually working her way down his torso. The guy was getting sexually aroused as the masseuse got closer to the towel. The towel began to rise, and the Swedish girl stopped her work and stood up. "You want a wank?" she asked. "You bet," came the excited reply. "OK," she said, "I come back in ten minutes."

Four men went golfing one day. Once on the course, three of them headed to the first tee and the fourth went into the clubhouse to take care of the bill. The three men started talking, bragging about their sons. The first man told the others, "My son is a builder and he is so successful that he gave a friend a brand new house for free."

The second man said, "My son is a car salesman and owns a huge dealership. He's so successful that he gave a friend a brand new BMW with all the extras." The third man, not wanting to be outdone, bragged, "My son is a stockbroker and he's doing so well that he gave his friend an entire stock portfolio worth £20 million."

It was at this point that the fourth man joined them on the tee. The first man mentioned, "We are just talking about our sons. How is yours doing?" The fourth man replied, "Well, my son is gay and dances in a gay bar." The three friends looked down at the grass and smirked. The fourth man carried on, "Admittedly, I'm not totally thrilled about the dancing job, but he must be doing pretty good. His last three boyfriends gave him a house, a brand new BMW, and a stock portfolio worth £20 million."

• • •

A man enters the confessional and says to the

Irish priest, "Father, it has been one month since my last confession. I have had sex with Fannie Green every week for the last month." The priest tells the sinner, "You are forgiven. Go out and say three Hail Marys."

Soon, another man enters the confessional. "Father, it has been two months since my last confession. I have had sex with Fannie Green twice a week for the last two months." This time the priest asks, "Who is "Fannie Green? " A new woman in the neighbourhood," the sinner replies. "Very well," says the priest, "go and say ten Hail Marys."

The next morning in church, the priest is preparing to deliver his sermon when suddenly a gorgeous, tall woman enters the church. All the men's eyes fall upon her as she slowly sashays up the aisle and sits down in front of the altar. Her dress is green and very short, with matching shiny emerald green shoes.

The priest and altar boy gasp, as the woman sits with her legs slightly spread apart. The priest turns to the altar boy and asks, "Is that Fannie Green?" The altar boy, whose eyes are popping out of his head, replies, "No Father, I think it's just the reflection off her shoes."

A world-famous golfer drives his BMW into a petrol station in a remote part of the countryside. The attendant at the pump greets him in a typically relaxed manner, completely unaware of the golf legend's identity. The golfer leans over to take the nozzle and, as he does so, two tees fall from his pocket.

Attendant: What are they then?
Golfer: They're called tees.
Attendant: Well, what on the good Earth are they for?
Gofer: They're for resting my balls on while I'm driving.
The attendant shakes his head. "By golly! Them fellas at BMW think of everything."

• • •

A young guy from Texas moves to California and goes to a big department store looking for a job. The manager says, "Do you have any sales experience?" The kid says, "Yeah, I was a salesman back home in Texas."

Well, the boss likes the kid so he gives him the job, saying, "You start tomorrow. I'll come down after we close and see how you did." At the end of the day, after the store is locked up, the boss comes down. "How many sales did you make today?" he asks. "One," says the kid. "One?" the boss says. "Just one? Our sales people average 20 or 30 sales a day. How much was the sale for?"

The kid says, "$101,237.64." The boss says, "$101,237.64? What the hell did you sell?" The kid says, "First I sold him a small fish hook. Then I sold him a medium fish hook. Then I sold him a larger fish hook. Then I sold him a new fishing rod. Then I asked him where he was going fishing and he said down at the coast, so I told him he was gonna need a boat, so we went down to the boat department and I sold him that twin engine Chris Craft. Then he said he didn't think his Honda Civic would pull it, so I took him down to the automotive department and sold him that 4 X 4 Blazer."

The boss says, "A guy came in here to buy a fish hook and you sold him a boat and truck as well?" "No," the kid replies, "he came in here to buy a box of tampons for his wife, and I said, "Well, your weekend's f**ked, you might as well go fishing."

• • •

Wife: What would you do if I died? Would you get married again?
Husband: Definitely not!
Wife: Why not – don't you like being married?

Husband: Of course I do.

Wife: Then why wouldn't you remarry?

Husband: Okay, I'd get married again.

Wife: You would?

Husband: (groan)

Wife: Would you sleep with her in our bed?

Husband: I've never even thought about it, but where else would we sleep?

Wife: Would you replace my pictures with hers?

Husband: I can't imagine why you're asking questions like this, but that would seem like the proper thing to do.

Wife: Would she use my golf clubs?

Husband: No, she's left-handed.

Wife: (silence)

Husband: (shit!)

• • •

Bob and his wife Laura are having marital problems and decide to see a sex therapist for help. The first thing the therapist says is, "Drop your pants. Let's have a look." The couple do as they're told and the therapist looks them up and down.

After a careful examination of both he says, "OK, I can help you two get that spark back in your marriage. Here's what you do. On your way home stop at the grocery store and buy a bag of grapes and a box of doughnuts. When you get home take off all of your clothes and sit on the floor facing each other across the room. Now Bob, you take the grapes, roll them across the floor one by one and try to get one in Laura's vagina.

When you get one in, crawl along the floor to her and retrieve the grape with your tongue. Laura, you take the doughnuts and play ring-toss with Bob. When you get one over his penis, crawl along the floor and slowly eat the doughnut. When you've done that, you'll have that spark you thought you'd lost."

Bob and Laura go home and try the therapy. To their surprise they have the best sex they've had in years!!! The next day Bob's friend Tom confides in him that he and his wife are having marital problems. Immediately Bob speaks up and says, "Tom, you have to go to this therapist. I guarantee he can help you! He really helped Laura and me."

So Tom takes his wife and goes to see the therapist. The first thing the therapist says is, "Drop your pants. Let's have a look at you both." Tom and his wife do as they're told and the therapist looks them up and down. Then he frowns and says, "I'm really sorry but there's nothing I can do for you." "WHAT!" yells Tom. "My friend Bob said that you could help us, guaranteed! Isn't there something you can do for us?" "Well," says the therapist, "OK, here's what you should do. On your way home, stop at the grocery store and pick up a bag of grapefruit and packet of Polos..."

• • •

A man and a woman who have never met before find themselves in the same sleeping carriage of a train. After the initial embarrassment, they both manage to get to sleep, the woman on the top bunk, the man on the lower. In the middle of the night, the woman leans over and says, "I'm sorry to bother you, but I'm awfully cold and I was wondering if you could possibly pass me another blanket."

The man leans out and, with a glint in his eye says, "I've got a better idea...let's pretend we're married." "Why not?" giggles the woman. "Good," he replies, "get your own f**king blanket."

• • •

A virile, young Italian soldier is relaxing at his favourite bar in Rome, when he manages to attract a spectacular young blonde. Things progress to the point where he invites her back to his apartment. They make small talk, then make love. After a pleasant interlude, he asks with a smile, "So, my darling...you finish?" She pauses for a second, frowns, and replies, "No."

Surprised, the young man reaches for her, and the lovemaking resumes. This time, she thrashes about wildly, and there are screams of passion. The lovemaking ends, and again the young man smiles and asks, "Thisa time you finish?" Again, she returns his smile, cuddles closer to him, and softly answers, "No."

Stunned, but damned if this woman is going to outlast him, the young man reaches for her. Using the last of his strength, he barely manages it, but they climax simultaneously, screaming, clawing and ripping bed sheets. The exhausted man falls on to his back, gasping. Barely able to turn his head, he looks into her eyes, smiles proudly, and asks, "So, you finnish?" "No!" she shouts back. "Stop asking me. I not finish, I Sveedish!"

• • •

A young couple was invited to a very upmarket masked Hallowe'en party. But a couple of hours before they were due to get ready, the wife came down with a terrible headache and told her husband to go to the party alone. As a considerate husband, he protested, but she insisted that it was bound to be a fun affair and said she was going to take some aspirin and go to bed. So he put his costume into a bag and set off in the car.

His wife, after sleeping soundly for an hour or so, woke to find that the pain was gone, and as it was still early, decided to go to the party after all. Because her husband didn't know what costume she had hired, she thought it would be fun to watch her husband to see how he acted when she was not around. She arrived at the party and soon spotted her husband cavorting around on the dance floor. He was dancing with every attractive woman he could, squeezing a boob here and stealing a little kiss there.

His wife worked her way through the throng and pushed in front of him. Having a rather voluptuous figure herself, he immediately devoted his time to this new 'babe'. She let him go as far as he wanted, as he was her husband, after all. Soon he whispered in her ear and she nodded, and taking him by the hand, led him outside to one of the cars where they screwed energetically. Just before the traditional 'unmasking' at midnight, she slipped out, went home and hid the costume before getting into bed. She couldn't wait to hear what kind of explanation he would have for his outrageous behaviour.

She was sitting up reading when he came in, and when he entered the bedroom, she asked him how the party had been. He replied, "Oh, the usual thing. You know I never really enjoy myself when you're not there." Then she asked, "Did you dance much?" "I never even had one dance," he sniffed. "When I got to the party, I met Jim, Bill and some of the other blokes, so we went into the den and played poker all evening. But you know what? You won't believe what happened to the guy I loaned my costume to!"

• • •

A woman decides to have a facelift for her 47th birthday. She spends £10,000 and feels pretty good about the results. On her way home she stops at a newsstand to buy a paper. Before leaving she asks the sale assistant, "I hope you don't mind my asking, but how old do you think I am?" "About 32," the assistant replies. "I'm actually 47!" the woman says happily.

A little while later she goes into a fast-food restaurant and asks the counter girl the same question. She replies, "I'd guess about 29." The woman replies, "Nope, I am 47!" Now she is feeling really good about herself. While waiting for the bus home, she asks an old man the same question. He replies, "I'm 78 and my eyesight is going. Although, when I was young, there was a sure way to tell how old a woman was, but it requires you to let me put my hands down your panties. Then, I can tell exactly how old you are."

They waited in silence on the empty street until curiosity got the best of the woman and she finally says, "What the hell – go ahead." The old man slips both hands down her panties and begins to feel around. After several minutes she says, "OK, how old am I?" He removes his hands slowly and says, "You are 47." Stunned, the woman says, "That is amazing. How do you know?" The old man replies, "I was behind you at the newsstand."

• • •

An old lady walked into the main branch of a major bank with £165,000 in a large bag. She asked to see the president of the bank as she wanted to deposit this money in a savings account, and was shown into his office. Curious, the president asked how she came by such a substantial sum.

"Making bets," replied the old lady. "What kind of bets?" he asked in amazement. "Well," she smiled, "for example, I'll bet you £25,000 that your testicles are square. Would you take that bet?" The president thought hard but couldn't see how he could lose. "Yes,' he replied. "I would take it."

The old lady stuck out her hand and said, "OK, but would you mind if I brought a lawyer with me tomorrow to witness the settling of the bet?" In view of the money involved, the president answered, "Of course not." At home that evening, the president stood naked in front of the mirror and looked at his balls from every possible angle, but couldn't see any way that they could be judged square.

The next day, the old lady returned with a distinguished-looking barrister and they were shown into the president's office. The old lady then asked the president to drop his trousers and underwear, which he did. She peered at his scrotum carefully, then asked, "Would you mind if I felt them?" The president, considering the money at stake, replied, "Not at all."

As she cupped his testicles in her hand, the president noticed the lawyer banging his head against the wall. "What on Earth are you doing?" he asked him. The old lady stood up and smiled.

"Yesterday I bet him £100,000 that today I would hold the balls of the president of any bank he chose in my hand."

• • •

A woman was having a passionate affair with an inspector from a pest-control company. One afternoon they were carrying on in the bedroom together when her husband arrived home unexpectedly. "Quick," said the woman to her lover, "into the closet!" And she pushed him in the closet, stark naked.

The husband, however, became suspicious, and after a search of the bedroom discovered the man

MUNCH! MUNCH!

in the closet. "Who are you?" he asked him. "I'm an inspector from Bugs-B-Gone," said the inspector. "What are you doing in there?" the husband asked. "I'm investigating a complaint about an infestation of moths," the man replied. "And where are your clothes?" asked the husband.

The man looked down at himself and said, "Those little bastards!"

• • •

A man and a woman start to have sex in the middle of a dark forest. After 15 minutes of activity, the man finally gets up and says, "Damn, I wish I had a flashlight." The woman says, "So do I. You've been eating grass for the past ten minutes!"

• • •

A woman and a baby were in the doctor's examining room, waiting for the doctor to come in for the baby's first examination. The doctor arrived, examined the baby, checked his weight, and being a little concerned, asked if the baby was breast-fed or bottle-fed.

"Breast-fed," she replied. "Well, strip down to your waist," the doctor ordered. He pinched her nipples, then pressed, kneaded, and rubbed both breasts for a while in a detailed examination. Motioning to her to get dressed, he said, "No wonder this baby is underweight. You don't have any milk." "I know," she said, "I'm his grandmother – but I'm glad I came."

• • •

One Friday, the boss stuck his head in Frank's office and told him that Frank would have to work late to finish an important report. Frank didn't mind but was concerned about letting his wife know that he would be late. They had recently moved, and the phone had yet to be installed. "No problem," said his boss, "I can go home that way and let her know."

A couple of hours later, the boss pulled up outside the house and knocked on the door. Frank's wife opened it wearing the flimsiest of negligees, and the boss felt a surge of testosterone. "May I come in a moment?" he asked. The wife stood back to let him pass and then closed the front door. She was gorgeous and he couldn't take his eyes off her. "I just stopped by to let you know that Frank will be late back today. Pardon me, but is there any chance of a f**k?"

"That's outrageous!" she gasped. "How dare you!" "Supposing I gave you fifty quid?" the boss asked. "Absolutely not!" she snapped. "One hundred pounds, then?" suggested the boss.

"Umm…no," she replied. "All right, two hundred and fifty-six pounds and eighty-five pence," he sighed. She hesitated, then whispered, "I don't think it would be right, do you?" He smiled, "Frank will never know and it will be the easiest two hundred and fifty quid you've ever earned. Plus we might both enjoy it. Then I'll be on my way."

She nodded and led him upstairs to the bedroom. Later that evening, Frank arrived home and found his wife in the kitchen. He gave her a hug and asked, "Did my boss come round to tell you that I'd be late?" "Oh yes," she answered, "he did pop by for a minute or two." "Oh good," smiled Frank, "then he gave you my wages too?"

• • •

An elderly man went to an old-timer's dance. He hadn't had any sex for a long time and had danced with almost every old woman in the place, but still hadn't scored. Feeling extremely frustrated, he approached an old grandma and said, "I'm having no luck with the other ladies here and I'm desperate for a f**k. How about coming back to my place for a roll in the hay? I'll give you 20 quid!"

She smiled and said, "I'm willing. Let's go." He couldn't believe his luck and took her back to his

place with mounting excitement. After a bit of foreplay, they headed for the bedroom.
Impatiently he tore of his clothes, then hers, and then mounted her with no further ado. The sex was great and he couldn't get over how tight she was for such an old woman.

After ten minutes of furious passion, he rolled off her and panted, "Wow! My dear, if I had known you were a virgin, I would have given you 50 quid!" Surprised, she replied, "If I had known you were actually going to manage an erection, I would have taken my tights off!"

• • •

Two deaf people get married. During the first week of marriage, they find they are unable to communicate in the bedroom when they turn the lights off, because they can't see each other using sign language. After several nights of confused fumbling and misunderstood intentions, the wife decides that they have to work out a system. "Sweetheart," she signs, "Why don't we agree on some simple signals? How about this: When we're in bed, if you want to have sex with me, reach over and squeeze my right breast once. If you don't want to have sex, reach over and squeeze my left breast once." The husband thinks this is a great idea and signs back to his wife, "Excellent! Now if you want to have sex

with me, reach over and pull on my penis once."
But if you don't want to have sex, reach over and
pull on my penis...oh, I don't know...shall we
say...fifty times?"

• • •

A woman is walking past a shop when she sees a
small poster in the window. It reads: 'Good
home wanted for clitoris licking frog'. She is
fascinated and goes into the shop and says to the
elegant man behind the counter, "I've come
about the clitoris licking frog." "Ah, oui.
Bonjour Madame," the assistant replies.

• • •

In the middle of an international gynaecology
conference, an English and a French
gynaecologist are discussing various cases
they've recently treated. The French
gynaecologist said. "Only last week, zere was a
woman ooh came to see me, and 'er cleetoris –
eet was like a melon." "Don't be absurd,"
sneered the English gynaecologist, "it couldn't
have been that big, my good man. She wouldn't
have been able to walk." The French
gynaecologist shrugged his shoulders, "Ah, you
Eenglish, zare you go again, always talkeeng
about ze size...I was talkeeng about ze flavour."

• • •

VERY RUDE JOKES

First-year students at medical school were receiving their first anatomy class with a dead human body. They all gathered around the surgery table with the body covered by a white sheet. The professor started the class by telling them, "It is necessary to have two important qualities as a doctor, and the first is that you should not be disgusted by anything involving the human body."

For an example, the professor pulled back the sheet, stuck his finger in the butt of the corpse, withdrew it and stuck it in his mouth. "Go ahead and do the same thing," he told his students. The students freaked out, hesitated for several minutes, but eventually took turns sticking a finger in the butt of the dead body and sucking on it. When everyone finished, the professor looked at the students and told them, "The second most important quality is observation - I stuck my middle finger in, and sucked on my index finger. Now learn to pay attention."

• • •

A skinny, timid accountant is sent to jail for embezzlement and is put in a cell with a huge, evil-looking bruiser. The big con says, "I want to have some sex. You wanna be the husband or the wife?" Thinking fast, the accountant replies, "Well, if I have to be one or the other, I guess I'd rather be the husband." "Good choice," grunts the giant thug. "Now get over here and suck your wife's dick."

A Petition I, the Penis, hereby request a raise in salary for the following reasons: I do physical labour. I work at great depths. I plunge head first into everything I do. I do not get weekends or public holidays off. I work in a damp environment. I don't get paid overtime. I work in a dark workplace that has poor ventilation. I work in high temperatures. My work exposes me to contagious diseases.

Dear Penis,
After assessing your request, and considering the arguments you have raised, the administration rejects your request for the following reasons: You do not work eight hours straight. You fall asleep on the job after brief work periods. You do not always follow the orders of the management team. You do not stay in your designated area and are often seen visiting other locations. You do not take initiative – you need to be pressured and stimulated in order to start working. You leave the workplace rather messy at the end of your shift. You don't always observe necessary safety regulations, such as wearing the correct protective clothing. You will retire well before you are 65. You are unable to work double shifts. You sometimes leave your designated work before you have completed the assigned task. And if that were not all, you have been seen constantly entering and exiting the workplace carrying two suspicious-looking bags.

Sincerely,

The Management

An executive was in a quandary. He had to get rid of one of his staff. He had narrowed it down to one of two people, Debra or Jack. It would be a hard decision to make, as they were both equally qualified and both did excellent work. He finally decided that in the morning whichever one used the water-cooler first would have to go.

Debra came in the next morning, hugely hung-over after partying all night. She went to the cooler to get some water to take an aspirin and the executive approached her and said, "Debra, I've never done this before, but I have to lay you or Jack off." Debra replied, "Could you jack off? I feel like shit."

• • •

A little boy who was curious about sex went to his father and asked him what a vagina looked like. His father smiled and said, "Well, Son, before sex, a vagina looks like a pink rose, with velvety leaves and the aroma of perfume." The boy asks, "What about after sex, Daddy?" The father replies, "After sex? Well, Son, have you ever seen a bulldog eating mayonnaise?"

• • •

A blind man walks into a restaurant and fumbles his way to a seat. The owner walks up to him and hands him a menu. "I'm sorry sir, but I'm blind and can't read a menu. Just bring me a dirty fork from a previous customer. I'll smell it and order from there." Puzzled, the owner walks into the kitchen and picks up a used fork. He returns to the blind man's table and hands it to him.

The blind man puts the fork to his nose and inhales deeply. "Ah, yes, that's what I'll have, gammon and mashed potatoes." The owner is amazed as he walks towards the kitchen. The cook happens to be the owner's wife and he tells her what has just happened. The blind man finishes his meal and leaves. Several days later he returns and the owner mistakenly brings him a menu again. "Excuse me, sir. You obviously don't remember me? I'm the blind man."

"I'm sorry," apologises the owner, "I didn't recognize you. I'll go get you a dirty fork." He comes back with another used fork and hands it to the blind man. After sniffing it, the blind man says, "That smells great. I'll take the pepperoni pizza with a salad and blue cheese dressing." Once again amazed, the owner decides that the blind man is screwing around with him and tells his wife that the next time the blind man comes in he's going to put him to the test. Shortly afterwards, the blind man clears his plate and leaves.

He returns a few days later, but this time the owner sees him coming and runs to the kitchen. He tells his wife, "Doris, rub this fork around your vagina before I take it to the blind man." Doris does so and hands her husband the fork. As the blind man takes his seat, the owner is ready and waiting. "Good afternoon, sir, this time I remembered you and I already have the fork ready for you." The blind man puts the fork to his nose, takes a long sniff and smiles, "Hey, I didn't know that Doris worked here!"

• • •

A man has a consultation with a plastic surgeon to arrange an operation on his penis. The surgeon has a careful look and asks, "What the hell happened to you, then?" The man sighs and says, "Well, I'm on holiday at a local caravan site, and the one next door was taken by a beautiful blonde all on her own. She's really gorgeous and obviously very horny, because most nights she takes a hot dog from the fridge and sticks it in a hole in the floor. Then she hitches up her skirt, squats down and humps the hot dog."

"So?" asks the surgeon. Embarrassed, the man explains, "It seemed like a real waste of top class pussy, so one evening I got under the trailer and waited. When she pushed the hot dog into the hole and started to lift her skirt, I pulled the hot dog out and stuck my dick there instead. Everything was going just dandy until someone knocked at her door. She jumped up and tried to kick the hot dog under the fridge."

• • •

An old lady dies and goes to heaven. She's chatting with St Peter at the Pearly Gates when all of a sudden she hears the most awful bloodcurdling screams. "Don't worry about that," says St Peter, "it's only someone having the holes bored into their shoulder blades for their wings." The old lady looks a little uncomfortable but carries on with the conversation.

Ten minutes later, there are more bloodcurdling screams. "Oh, my God," says the old lady, "now what is happening?" "Not to worry," says St Peter, "they are just having their head drilled to fit the halo." "I can't do this," says the old lady, "I'm off to hell." "You mustn't go there," says St Peter, "you'll be raped and sodomized." "Yes, maybe," she says, "but I've already got the holes for that!"

• • •

Several years ago, Great Britain funded a study to determine why the head of a man's penis is larger than the shaft. The study took two years and cost over £180,000. The results concluded that the reason the head of a man's penis is larger than the shaft is to provide the man with more pleasure during sex.

After the results were published, the French declared that the British were wrong and decided to conduct their own study of the same subject. After three years of research and a cost in excess of 250,000 Euros, they concluded that the head of a man's penis is larger than the shaft to provide the woman with more sexual pleasure.

When the results of the French study were released, Australia decided to conduct its own study. So, after nearly three weeks of intensive research and a cost of around Aus$75, the Aussie's study was complete. They came to the conclusion that the reason the head of a man's penis is larger than the shaft is to prevent his hand from flying off and hitting him in the forehead.

• • •

Three boy scouts, a lawyer, a priest and a pilot are in a plane that is about to crash. The pilot says, "I'm afraid that we only have three parachutes. Let's give them to the three boy scouts. They are young and have their whole lives in front of them." The lawyer yells, "F**k the boy scouts!" The priest frowns and says, "Surely there's too little time?"

An old man goes to the doctor for his yearly physical, his wife tagging along. When the doctor enters the examination room, he tells the old man, "I need a urine sample, a stool sample and a sperm sample."

The old man, being hard of hearing, looks at his wife and yells, "What? What did he say? What does he want?" His wife yells back, "He needs your underwear."

• • •

There was a guy who was struggling to decide what to wear to go to a swingers' fancy dress party...then he had a bright idea. When the host answered the door, he found the guy standing there with no shirt and no socks on. "What the hell are you supposed to be?" asked the host. "A premature ejaculation," said the man. "I just came in my pants!"

• • •

A nun gets into a taxi, and after a few minutes the cab driver starts staring at her in the rear-view mirror. A little later he says, "I hope you don't find this offensive, but my biggest fantasy is to be sucked off by a nun." The nun smiles and replies, "I don't find it offensive. I've often wondered what it would be like to do that. However, I have two conditions. You have to be single and a good catholic."

The taxi driver pulls over and climbs in the back. "Oh, yes!" he pants, "I'm both of those." "Well, all right then," the nun smiles as she slides down. When she has finished, she sits up, and the cab driver, his passion spent, feels a wave of shame. "I'm so sorry. I'm really a married man and I'm not even a catholic at all." The nun smiles and replies, "Well, don't worry about it. My real name's Danny, and I'm on my way to a fancy dress party."

• • •

A dustman is going along a street picking up the wheelie bins and emptying them into his dustcart lorry. He gets to a house where the bin hasn't been left out, so he has a quick look for it round the back. He still can't see it, so he knocks on the door. There's no answer so he knocks again. Eventually a Japanese bloke answers...

"Harro," he says. "All right mate, where's your bin?" asks the dustman. "I bin on toilet," replies the Japanese bloke, looking perplexed. Realising the Japanese fellow has misunderstood, the dustman smiles and says, "No mate, where's your dust bin?" "I dust bin on toilet having shit," says the Japanese man. "Mate," says the dustman, "you're misunderstanding me...where's your wheelie bin?" "OK, OK," sighs the Japanese fellow, "I wheelie bin having wank."

There were four nuns in line for confessional, and the first nun said, "Forgive me, Father, for I have sinned." He asked how. She replied, "I saw a man's cock." He told her to wash her eyes with holy water. The second nun came in and said, "Forgive me, Father, for I have sinned." When he asked how, she answered, "I touched a man's cock." He told her to wash her hands in holy water. Then he heard the third and fourth nun fighting. He asked why they were behaving in such an undignified fashion, and the fourth nun grumbled, "I'm not going to wash my mouth in the holy water if she is going to sit in it."

• • •

A young couple are snuggled up in the back row of the cinema. Suddenly the girl says, "I really need a piss, can I squeeze past you?"

"Why don't you just squat down on the floor and do it," says the boyfriend, "you'll disturb all these people. Besides its dark, no one will see you." "OK," she says, and then pulls her drawers down and squats on the floor. The bloke starts feeling very horny at the thought of her down there, so he reaches down between her legs and extends his finger. He feels something long, warm and quite firm, and says, "Urgh! You're not a transvestite are you?" "Of course not," she says, "I've just changed my mind...I'm having a shit instead."

DEFINITIONS

What is the definition of confidence?

When your wife catches you in bed with another woman and you slap her on the ass and say, "You're next!"

What's the difference between a whore and a bitch?

A whore sleeps with everybody at the party, and a bitch sleeps with everybody at the party except you.

What's the difference between love, true love and showing off?

Spitting, swallowing and gargling.

What three words do you dread most while making love?

"Honey, I'm home."

What did the cannibal do after he dumped his girlfriend?

Wipe his arse.

What do the gynaecologist and the pizza deliveryman have in common?

They both get to smell the goods but neither one can eat it.

What do you call a prostitute with a runny nose?

Full.

How is pubic hair like parsley?
You push it to the side before you start eating.

Why are women and takeaway fried chicken the same?
By the time you're finished with the breast and thighs, all you have left is the greasy box to put your bone in.

How are tornadoes and marriage alike?
They both begin with a lot of sucking and blowing, but in the end you lose your house.

What's the difference between getting a divorce and getting circumcised?
When you get a divorce, you get rid of the whole prick!

When is a pixie not a pixie?
When he's got his head up a fairy's skirt – then he's a-goblin'.

Which of the following is the odd one out: wife, meat, eggs, blow job?
The blow job. You can beat your wife, your meat and your eggs, but you just can't beat a blow job.

What's the difference between a blonde and an ironing board?
It's difficult to open the legs of an ironing board.

What have women and condoms got in common?

Both spend more time in your wallet than on the end of your dick.

Who is the most popular guy at the nudist colony?

The one who can carry a cup of coffee in each hand and a dozen doughnuts.

Who is the most popular girl at the nudist colony?
She is the one who can eat the last doughnut!

Do you know why they call it the Wonder Bra?
When you take it off you wonder where her tits went.

• • •

An attractive but scruffy blonde entered a run-down bar and asked for a lager. She took it from the barman, glugged it down, then swayed and passed out cold. "Someone gimme a hand," grunted the barman. A couple of the regulars helped him carry the unconscious girl into a back room. They laid her on a couch and stood looking down at her.

One of the men whispered, "Hey guys, why don't we pork her. No one will know and she'll certainly never notice." They didn't take much persuading, and an hour later they were back in the bar when she woke up, straightened her clothes and wandered out into the street.

They next day there were a few more drinkers at the bar when she re-appeared and asked for a lager. As before, she downed it in one, swayed, then crumpled to the floor. The barman and seven others carried her into the back room and took it in turns to f**k her. An hour later she staggered out and disappeared up the street.

When she entered the bar the next day, there were 18 men watching as she ordered a lager. Sure enough, no sooner had she drained the glass than she slumped to the floor. All 18 men took it in turns to empty their tanks.

By the following day word had really travelled, and there were 26 men eagerly awaiting her arrival. Sure enough, in she came and walked up to the bar. "Pint of lager?" asked the barman with a welcoming smile. "Nah," she frowned, "I'll have a gin. Lager gives me a pain in the c**t."

• • •

It was a nice sunny day, and three men were walking down a country road, when they saw a bush with a pig's arse sticking out from it. The first man sighs, "I wish that was Jordan's arse!" The second man says, "I wish that was Pamela Anderson's arse." Then the third man quietly murmured, "I wish it was dark."

• • •

A man is lying in bed with his wife, reading a book. He reaches down under the sheet and inserts his finger in her pussy. "Do you feel like some sex, Sweetheart?" she asks. "No thanks, Dear," he replies, "I'm just wetting my finger to turn the page!"

• • •

When the time came to leave for work, a man kissed his beautiful wife, left his house, climbed into his Jag and set off for the office. Two miles down the road he remembered that he'd left an important file in the bedroom. He did a U-turn and headed back home.

When he opened the bedroom door he saw his wife lying on the bed, totally nude. Standing beside the bed was the milkman, also naked, who suddenly squatted down on the floor. He looked up as the furious husband took a step towards him and said, "I'm very glad you're here, Mr Fanshaw. I was just telling your wife that if she doesn't settle her f**king milk bill, I'm going to shit all over the carpet."

• • •

A woman is driving through the woods of Kentucky when she is forced to slam on the brakes as a coyote runs across the road in front of her. Just as she regains her wits and gets ready to carry on her way, a woodsman runs right in front of her, catches the coyote by the hind legs and starts f**king it. "Oh my God!" she exclaims and speeds into the nearest town to find the local lawman. The sheriff's car is parked in front of the town bar, so she storms inside. The first thing she sees is a very old man with a long white beard sitting in the corner jacking off. Shocked, she rushes up to the sheriff who's sitting at the bar with his drink. "What kind of sick town is this? she says. "The first thing I see is a man sodomising a beast in full view. And just look at that disgusting old man in the corner jacking off in public! Aren't you going to do anything about it?" "Well, ma'am," drawls the sheriff, "you surely don't expect him to catch a coyote at his age, do ya?"

Two nuns were driving along in their ancient Morris Minor and stopped at a set of lights. Immediately, a scruffy individual rushed over and started cleaning their windscreen. "Go away!" shouted the junior sister. But the man continued unabashed. "Leave us alone!" demanded the Mother Superior to no effect. "Why don't you show him your cross?" suggested the young nun. "Good idea," nodded the senior nun. She wound down the window and yelled, "F**k off, you cock-sucking little c**t!"

• • •

One day a coroner came out his lab to talk to his boss about the body he was attending to. "Uh, boss," he said, "in all my years working here I've seen some pretty strange things but nothing as bad as what I have in the lab." "What's wrong?" asked his boss. The coroner scratched his head. "There's this really obese woman with a shrimp stuck in her vagina."

"What!!! Are you sure?" queried his boss. "Yeah! Go check it out for yourself," came the reply. The senior man walked into the lab and took a look. "You complete idiot," he laughed. "That's not a shrimp – it's her clitoris." "Are you sure?" asked the coroner. "It sure tasted like shrimp."

A husband wakes up one Saturday morning, looks out of the window and says, "What a beautiful, sunny morning." He turns to his wife. "Darling, we're going fishing this weekend. Just you, me and the dog." His wife frowns and grumbles, "But I don't like fishing!" Her husband pulls on his clothes and replies, "Look! We're going fishing and that's that." His wife continues to protest and her husband shouts, "Right! You've got three choices: One, you come fishing with me and the dog; Two, you give me a blow job; or Three, you take it up the arse!"

His wife grimaces, "But I don't want to do any of those things!" Her husband pulls back the bedclothes and insists, "Look. I've given you three options. You HAVE to do one of them! I'm going to the garage to sort out my fishing gear, and when I come back I expect you to have made up your mind!" The woman sits and thinks about it until her husband returns and snaps, "Well? What have you decided? Fishing, blow job or arse?"

His wife sees that he is not going to give in and finally makes up her mind, "OK. I'll give you a blow job!" "Great!" he says and drops his pants. The wife gets on her knees and starts. Suddenly she stops, looks up at her husband, and says, "It tastes horrible. It tastes like shit!" "I'm not surprised," mumbles her husband, "the dog didn't want to go fishing either."

• • •

A man becomes concerned about his wife's growing forgetfulness and consults his local GP as to the best course of action. The doctor considers the symptoms for a while then says, "Well, it's either Alzheimer's disease or advanced syphilis." "What makes you say that?" says the shocked husband, "can't you tell the difference?"
The doctor explains, "Well, you see, at certain

stages of each disease they have symptoms in common, and it's extremely hard to tell which it is." The husband asks what he can do about the situation. "Tell you what," says the doctor, "take her for a nice long drive into the country and push her out of the car. If she manages to find her way back, don't f**k her any more."

• • •

Three women were sitting in a bar discussing how much their husbands could fit into their vaginas. The first women said proudly, "My husband can get his whole hand up me." The second said, "My husband can get his whole head up me." The third woman smiled, spread her legs and slid down the shaft of the barstool.

• • •

Three middle-aged women are walking down the street when a man conducting a survey stops them. He asks, "Ladies, would you mind telling me how you know if you've had a good night out?" The first replies, "I come home, get into bed and if I lay there and tingle all over, I know that I had a good night."

The second one replies, "I come home, have a shower and a glass of wine, get into bed, and if my fanny feels warm, I know it was a good night." The third one turns round and says, "If I get home, rip off me knickers, throw them against the wall, and they stick, then I know it was a good night!"

• • •

A lonesome miner finally struck a good vein of gold after months spent in backbreaking solitude high up in the hills of Alaska. Whooping with joy, he came down from the mountains and walked into a saloon in the nearest town. "I'm lookin' for the meanest, roughest and toughest whore in the Yukon!" he bellowed to the bartender. "We got her!" replied the barman. "She's upstairs in the second room on the right."

The miner handed the bartender a gold nugget to pay for the whore and two beers. He grabbed the bottles, stomped up the stairs, kicked open the second door and yelled, "I'm lookin' for the meanest, roughest and toughest whore in the Yukon!" The woman sitting naked on the bed looked at the miner and said, "Well, old timer, you've found her!" In seconds she stripped naked, bent over and grabbed her ankles. "How did you know I want to do it like that?" asked the miner.

"I didn't," replied the whore, "I just thought you might like to open those beers first."

THE END